The
GOOD COOK'S
Book of Days

GLOSSARY OF INGREDIENTS AND TECHNIQUES

Al dente: Just firm to the bite, the correct texture for pasta and some vegetables.

Baste: To moisten meat or vegetables during cooking.

Blind baking: This term refers to the baking of a pastry case prior to filling it. To bake blind, line the pastry with a sheet of baking paper or aluminium foil. Weigh it down with dried beans, uncooked rice or pasta. The quantity of beans, rice or pasta should be enough to compensate for the filling and be pushed well out to the edges so that the sides are supported. Bake the pastry case at 200°C/400°F/Gas 6 for 10 minutes or as directed in the recipe. Remove lining and weights and bake pastry case for 7-10 minutes longer or until pastry is cooked through and lightly browned. Cool pastry before filling. Allow beans, rice or pasta to cool completely, then store in an airtight container for future use. Do not use for any other purpose.

Blending: Mixing a liquid such as water with a dry ingredient such as cornflour. The mixture should be smooth and well combined.

Bind: To hold dry ingredients together with egg or liquid.

Bouillon: Broth or uncleared stock.

Bouquet garni: A small bunch of herbs, usually parsley, thyme and a bay leaf. A bouquet garni is added to stews, soups or stocks for flavouring. Commercially prepared sachets of dried herbs are also available from supermarkets.

Buttermilk: This is a cultured dairy product that has the same food value as skim milk. It is a useful low-fat ingredient that is somethimes used in baked goods.

Clarify: To melt and strain butter of its milk particles and impurities. Also means to clear stocks and jellies by filtering. To clarify butter, place it in a small saucepan and melt it over a medium heat. Skim the foam from the surface of the butter, then slowly pour the butter into a bowl, leaving behind the milky-white solids. Ghee, which is used in Indian cooking is a type of clarified butter.

Flake: To separate cooked or canned fish flesh into small pieces.

Fold in: To combine ingredients quickly and gently without deflating what is usually a light mixture. A large metal spoon or spatula is ideal for doing this.

Kneading: This is usually done on a lightly floured surface. The hands or fingertips are used to turn the outside edge of a mixture into the centre. Do this to either shape a mixture into a ball (pastry) or to alter the nature of the mixture by working with your hands (bread dough).

Parboil: To boil for part of the cooking time before finishing by another method.

Poach: To cook by simmering very gently in liquid.

Reduce: To concentrate or thicken a liquid by rapid boiling.

Refresh: To rinse freshly cooked vegetables in cold water to stop the cooking process and set the colour, usually with green vegetables.

Roux: A blend of melted butter and flour, cooked as a base for thickening sauces and soups.

Scald: To heat liquid, usually milk, to just below boiling point.

Sear: To brown meat, quickly on a hot surface to retain juices.

Segment: To cut the peel and all the white pith from citrus fruit, then cut between the membranes joining the segments.

Skim: To remove scum or fat from the surface of a liquid.

Tuile Cups with White Chocolate (pg 81)

january
janvier

januar
enero

1	8	15
2	9	16
3	10	17
4	11	18
5	12	19
6	13	20
7	14	21

22	29
23	30
24	31
25	
26	
27	
28	

SENSATIONAL SOUPS

When serving soup as a starter, allow about 1 cup/250 mL/8 fl oz of soup per person.

Soup develops a better flavour if made a day in advance.

Soups can be stored in an airtight container in the refrigerator for up to 2 days.

Soups can be frozen in an airtight container for up to 3 months.

When freezing any liquid, leave a 5 cm/2 in space between the liquid and the lid of the container as liquid expands during freezing.

Thaw frozen soup by placing it in the refrigerator ovenight – do not leave it at room temperature to defrost as this may lead to the growth of bacteria which causes food poisoning. Alternatively thaw it in the microwave on HIGH (100%) allowing 5-8 minutes for each 4 cups/1 litre/1¾ pt of soup. Stir once or twice so that the soup thaws evenly. Thaw fish and seafood soups on DEFROST (30%).

ORIENTAL NOODLE SOUP
Serves 4

4 cups/1 litre/1³/₄ pt vegetable stock
¹/₂ cup/125 mL/4 fl oz tamari
250 g/8 oz bean thread noodles
375 g/12 oz tofu, roughly chopped
155 g/5 oz bok choy, chopped
1 stalk fresh lemon grass, chopped, or
1 tspn dried lemon grass, soaked in hot water
until soft or 1 tspn finely grated lemon rind
3 spring onions, sliced diagonally
5 cm/2 in piece fresh ginger, sliced
200 g/6¹/₂ oz straw or button mushrooms
1 tblspn chopped fresh mint
2 tblspn chopped fresh coriander
100 g/3¹/₂ oz bean sprouts

1 Place stock and tamari in a large saucepan and bring to the boil. Reduce heat, add noodles, tofu, bok choy, lemon grass or lemon rind, spring onions, ginger, mushrooms, mint and coriander and simmer for 20 minutes.

2 To serve, divide bean sprouts between four warmed serving bowls and ladle over hot soup.

CARROT AND ORANGE SOUP
Serves 4

1 tblspn vegetable oil
2 leeks, thinly sliced
6 large carrots, sliced
2 tblspn curry powder
1 tblspn finely grated lemon rind
1 cup/250 mL/8 fl oz orange juice
1¹/₂ cups/375 mL/12 fl oz coconut milk
2 cups/500 mL/16 fl oz vegetable stock
freshly ground black pepper
¹/₃ cup/60 g/2 oz natural yogurt
100g/3¹/₂ oz cashews, roasted and chopped
1 tblspn chopped fresh mint

1 Heat oil in a large saucepan. Add leeks and cook over a medium heat, stirring, for 5 minutes or until golden. Add carrots, curry powder, lemon rind and orange juice, bring to the boil and simmer for 10 minutes or until carrots are soft.

2 Stir in coconut milk and stock and simmer for 10 minutes longer.

3 Remove pan from heat and set aside to cool slightly. Place soup mixture, in batches, in a food processor or blender and process until smooth.

4 Return soup to a clean saucepan and heat over a medium heat, stirring for 4-5 minutes or until hot. Season to taste with black pepper. Serve soup topped with yogurt, cashews and mint.

SWEET POTATO AND LEEK SOUP
Serves 4-6

1 kg/2 lb orange sweet potatoes, cut
into large pieces
2 onions, halved
2 leeks, halved
4 cups/1 litre/1³/4 pt chicken stock
2 cups/500 mL/16 fl oz water
1 tspn ground cumin
freshly ground black pepper
sour cream
fresh mint sprigs

1 Place sweet potatoes, onions and leeks in a well-oiled baking dish and bake at 200°C/400°F/Gas 6 for 45 minutes or until tender. Cool slightly.

2 Place baked vegetables, stock, water, cumin and black pepper to taste, in batches, in a food processor or blender and process until smooth.

3 Place soup in a saucepan, bring to simmering over a medium heat and simmer, stirring occasionally, for 3-4 minutes or until hot. Serve garnished with sour cream and mint sprigs.

HOT AND SPICY PRAWN SOUP
Serves 4

4 cups/1 litre/1³/₄ pt fish stock
5 cm/2 in piece fresh galangal, sliced or
8 pieces dried galangal
8 kaffir lime leaves
2 stalks fresh lemon grass, finely chopped or
1 tspn dried lemon grass, soaked in
hot water until soft
2 tblspn lime juice
2 tblspn finely sliced lime rind
2 tblspn Thai fish sauce
2 tblspn Thai red curry paste
500 g/1 lb large uncooked prawns, shelled and
deveined, tails left intact
3 spring onions, sliced diagonally
3 tblspn fresh coriander leaves
1 small fresh red chilli, sliced

1 Place stock in a large saucepan and bring to the boil over a medium heat. Add galangal, lime leaves, lemon grass, lime juice, lime rind, fish sauce and curry paste and simmer, stirring occasionally, for 10 minutes.

2 Add prawns and spring onions and simmer for 5 minutes or until prawns are cooked. Remove galangal and discard. Serve soup sprinkled with coriander leaves and sliced chilli.

VEGETABLE SOUP WITH PISTOU
Serves 6

1 tblspn olive oil
2 onions, chopped
2 leeks, sliced
1 tspn chopped fresh thyme or
$^1/_2$ tspn dried thyme
3 stalks celery, sliced
2 large potatoes, diced
2 carrots, diced
2 zucchini (courgettes), sliced
250 g/8 oz green beans, sliced
440 g/14 oz canned lima, butter, red kidney
or mixed beans, drained
8 cups/2 litres/$3^1/_2$ pt water
freshly ground black pepper
PISTOU
1 bunch fresh basil, leaves removed and
stems discarded
2 cloves garlic, chopped
125 g/4 oz fresh Parmesan cheese, chopped
$^1/_4$ cup/60 mL/2 fl oz olive oil

1 Heat 1 tblspn olive oil in a large saucepan over a medium heat, add onions, leeks and thyme and cook, stirring, for 5 minutes or until onions and leeks are soft.

2 Add celery, potatoes and carrots and cook, stirring, for 5 minutes. Add zucchini (courgettes), green beans, canned beans and water and bring to the boil. Reduce heat and simmer for 30 minutes or until vegetables are tender. Season to taste with black pepper.

3 Pistou: Place basil leaves, garlic, Parmesan cheese, $^1/_4$ cup/60 mL/2 fl oz olive oil and black pepper to taste in a food processor or blender and process to make a paste. Just prior to serving, stir Pistou into soup.

GARLIC AND PARSLEY SOUP
Serves 6

1 head garlic, cloves separated and unpeeled
6 cups/1.5 litres/$2^1/_2$ pt chicken or
vegetable stock
$^1/_4$ tspn dried sage
$^1/_4$ tspn dried thyme
1 small bay leaf
3 sprigs fresh parsley
2 large potatoes, diced
pinch saffron powder
1 bunch fresh parsley, finely chopped
freshly ground black pepper

1 Blanch garlic cloves in boiling water for 30 seconds. Drain, rinse under cold water and peel.

2 Place garlic, stock, sage, thyme, bay leaf and parsley sprigs in a large saucepan and bring to the boil. Reduce heat and simmer for 30 minutes.

3 Add potatoes and saffron to stock mixture and simmer for 15-20 minutes or until potatoes are tender. Discard bay leaf. Cool slightly.

4 Place soup in batches in a food processor or blender and process until smooth. Return soup to a clean saucepan, bring to the boil and simmer for 2-3 minutes or until soup is hot. Stir in chopped parsley and season to taste with black pepper.

Vegetable Soup with Pistou, Garlic and Parsley Soup

february
février
februar
febrero

1	8	15
2	9	16
3	10	17
4	11	18
5	12	19
6	13	20
7	14	21

22	29
23	
24	
25	
26	
27	
28	

SHORTCUTS

Time saving starts with a well organised kitchen. Keeping work surfaces free and having all your utensils to hand makes life easier.

Keep a selection of bread and rolls in the freezer. They defrost quickly and are a good accompaniment to any meal.

Bottled minced garlic, ginger and chillies are available from supermarkets. These save having to crush, chop and mince when time is short.

Cooked rice and pasta freeze well, they reheat in minutes in the microwave and save time on busy nights.

For quicker preparation, buy products that are partly prepared – cubed meat, grated cheese, instant (no precooking required) lasagne and boned chicken. Many supermarkets and greengrocers also sell fresh salads and vegetables mixes for soups and casseroles.

SALMON FRITTATA
Serves 4

4 eggs, lightly beaten
$1/2$ cup/125 mL/4 fl oz milk
2 tspn wholegrain mustard
freshly ground black pepper
2 tspn vegetable oil
4 spring onions, chopped
220 g/7 oz canned pink or red salmon, drained
2 tspn finely grated lemon rind

1 Place eggs, milk, mustard and black pepper to taste in a bowl and whisk to combine. Heat oil in a nonstick frying pan over a medium heat, add spring onions and cook, stirring, for 1 minute. Add salmon and lemon rind and spread evenly over base of pan.

2 Pour egg mixture into pan and cook over a low heat for 5 minutes or until frittata is set. Place pan under a preheated hot grill and cook for 3-4 minutes or until top is golden.

BURGERS WITH A LOT
Serves 6

500 g/1 lb lean beef mince
³/₄ cup/45 g/1¹/₂ oz wholemeal breadcrumbs,
made from stale bread
1 egg, lightly beaten
1 tblspn chopped fresh parsley
1 tblspn vegetable oil
6 wholegrain rolls, halved and toasted
4 tblspn tomato relish
6 lettuce leaves
60 g/2 oz alfalfa sprouts
1 raw beetroot, peeled and grated
6 slices Emmental cheese

1 Combine beef, breadcrumbs, egg and parsley and shape into six patties.

2 Heat oil in a frying pan over a medium heat, add patties and cook for 3 minutes each side or until cooked to your liking.

3 Spread bottom halves of rolls with tomato relish and top each with a pattie, a lettuce leaf, some alfalfa sprouts, some beetroot, a slice of cheese and top half of roll.

HOT HAM SANDWICHES

Serves 4

**2 x 10 cm/4 in squares focaccia bread or
2 small French bread sticks
185 g/6 oz ricotta cheese, drained
250 g/8 oz smoked ham, sliced
60 g/2 oz sun-dried tomatoes, sliced
3 tblspn chopped fresh basil
30 g/1 oz fresh Parmesan cheese shavings**

Split focaccia bread or French bread sticks horizontally and spread each half with ricotta cheese. Top with ham, sun-dried tomatoes, basil and Parmesan cheese shavings. Place under a preheated hot grill and cook for 3-4 minutes or until cheese melts and is golden.

GRILLED BANANA SANDWICHES

Serves 4

**8 slices rye or Granary bread
2 bananas, sliced
1 avocado, sliced
8 slices Gruyére cheese**

Place bread under a preheated hot grill and cook for 2-3 minutes or until toasted on one side. Top untoasted side with bananas, avocado and cheese. Place under grill and cook for 3-4 minutes longer or until cheese melts and is golden.

HOT CHICKEN SANDWICHES
Serves 4

8 slices wholemeal or white bread, toasted
4 tblspn mayonnaise
500 g/1 lb cooked chicken, skin removed
and flesh shredded
440 g/14 oz canned asparagus spears, drained
freshly ground black pepper
8 slices Swiss cheese, such as
Emmental or Gruyére

Spread toast with mayonnaise and top with chicken, asparagus, black pepper to taste and cheese. Place under a preheated hot grill and cook for 3-4 minutes or until cheese melts and is golden.

BANANA SMOOTHIE
Makes 1

1 banana, peeled
$^1/_2$ cup/125 mL/4 fl oz cold milk
$^1/_2$ cup/100 g/3$^1/_2$ oz natural or
fruit-flavoured yogurt of your choice
pinch ground nutmeg

1 Place banana, milk and yogurt in food processor or blender and process for 20-30 seconds or until thick and smooth.

2 Pour into glass, sprinkle with nutmeg and serve immediately.

NEW YORK BAGEL
Serves 4

4 poppy seed bagels, split
90 g/3 oz cottage cheese
freshly ground black pepper
$^1/_2$ bunch/125 g/4 oz watercress,
broken into sprigs
185 g/6 oz rare roast beef, thinly sliced
1 avocado, halved, stoned and thinly sliced
4 tblspn spicy tomato relish

1 Spread bottom half of each bagel with cottage cheese and season to taste with black pepper.

2 Top with watercress sprigs, beef, avocado, relish and top half of bagel.

SUN-DRIED TOMATO DIP
Serves 4

250 g/8 oz sun-dried tomatoes
60 g/2 oz pine nuts
3 tblspn chopped fresh basil
3 tblspn grated fresh Parmesan cheese
250 g/8 oz cream cheese, softened
bagel chips or French bread, sliced
selection of raw vegetables such as cherry
tomaotes, celery sticks, carrot sticks, broccoli
florets, cauliflower florets and green beans

Place sun-dried tomatoes, pine nuts, basil, Parmesan cheese and cream cheese in a food processor or blender and process until smooth. Place dip in a bowl on a serving platter or tray and surround with bagel chips or bread and/or raw vegetables.

march
mars
márz
mars

1	8	15
2	9	16
3	10	17
4	11	18
5	12	19
6	13	20
7	14	21

22	29
23	30
24	31
25	
26	
27	
28	

FISH FACTS

Oily fish such as salmon, tuna and mackerel have more Omega-3 fatty acids than white fish. Medical research shows that Omega-3 has a lowering effect on blood pressure and blood fats.

When buying fish fillets, look for those that are shiny and firm with a pleasant sea smell. Avoid fillets that are dull, soft, discoloured or 'ooze' water when touched.

When buying whole fish look for those that have bright, full eyes, bright red gills and a bright, glossy skin.

When storing prawns, leave them in their shell. The shells act as an insulator and help retain moisture and flavour. Cooked prawns should be stored in the refrigerator in an airtight container or plastic food bag for no longer than 3 days. Uncooked prawns are best stored in the refrigerator in water in an airtight container for up to 3 days. The water prevents oxidation.

FISH AND CHIPS
Serves 4

500 g/1 lb oven fries
vegetable oil for shallow-frying
4 boneless firm white fish fillets

BEER BATTER
1 cup/125 g/4 oz flour
2 egg whites, lightly beaten
³/4 cup/185 mL/6 fl oz beer
1 tblspn vegetable oil

1 Batter: Place flour in a bowl and make a well in the centre. Add egg whites, beer and 1 tblspn vegetable oil and mix until smooth.

2 Cook oven fries according to packet directions.

3 Heat 5 cm/2 in vegetable oil in a frying pan over a medium heat until a cube of bread dropped in browns in 50 seconds. Dip fish in batter, add to pan and cook for 3 minutes each side or until golden. Drain on absorbent kitchen paper. Serve with oven fries.

PEPPERED SALMON
Serves 4

4 salmon cutlets
30 g/1 oz butter

BLACK PEPPER MARINADE
2 tblspn coarsely cracked black peppercorns
2 tblspn chopped fresh dill
2 tblspn lemon juice

LIME YOGURT
2 tblspn snipped fresh chives
2 tblspn lime juice
1 tblspn finely grated lime rind
2 tspn honey
1¹/₄ cups/250 g/8 oz low-fat natural yogurt

1 Lime Yogurt: Combine chives, lime juice, lime rind, honey and yogurt. Chill.

2 Marinade: Place black peppercorns, dill and lemon juice in plastic food bag. Add salmon and shake to coat. Marinate for 5 minutes.

3 Melt butter in a frying pan over a medium heat, add salmon and cook for 2-3 minutes or until fish flakes when tested with a fork. Serve with Lime Yogurt.

FISH EN PAPILLOTE
Serves 4

4 red snapper or bream fillets
1 egg white, lightly beaten
1 carrot, cut into thin strips
1 leek, cut into thin strips
1 red pepper, cut into thin strips
4 sprigs fresh lemon thyme or thyme
freshly ground black pepper

HERB MARINADE
2 tblspn olive oil
1 tblspn white wine vinegar
1 tblspn finely chopped fresh dill
1 tblspn snipped fresh chives

1 Marinade: Combine oil, vinegar, dill and chives in a small bowl. Place fish in a shallow glass or ceramic dish, pour over marinade, cover and marinate for 2 hours. Drain well.

2 Cut four circles of nonstick baking paper large enough to completely enclose the fillets. The paper should be at least 10 cm/4 in larger than the fillets on all sides. Fold paper in half lengthwise and cut a half-heart shape. Open out paper and brush edges with egg white.

3 Place a fillet on one half of each paper heart, near the centre fold line, then top with carrot, leek, red pepper, a sprig of thyme and black pepper to taste. Fold other half of paper over ingredients and roll edges to seal. Place paper parcels on a baking tray and bake at 200°C/400°F/Gas 4 for 20 minutes or until fish flakes when tested with a fork.

SEAFOOD WITH GREEN VEGETABLES
Serves 4

100 g/3¹/₂ oz snow peas (mangetout)
250 g/8 oz broccoli, broken into small florets
250 g/8 oz asparagus spears, trimmed
1¹/₂ cups/375 mL/12 fl oz fish stock
250 g/8 oz large uncooked prawns, shelled
and deveined, tails intact
250 g/8 oz boneless firm white fish fillets,
cut into 2 cm/³/₄ in cubes
250 g/8 oz scallops
¹/₂ cup/125 mL/4 fl oz cream (double)
¹/₄ cup/60 mL/2 fl oz tomato purée
1 tblspn chopped fresh tarragon or
1 tspn dried tarragon
freshly ground black pepper

1 Steam or microwave snow peas (mangetout), broccoli and asparagus, separately, until just tender. Drain and refresh under cold running water. Set aside.

2 Place stock in a large saucepan and bring to the boil, add prawns, fish and scallops to stock and cook for 5 minutes or until just cooked. Using a slotted spoon remove and set aside.

3 Stir in cream, tomato purée and tarragon and bring to the boil. Reduce heat and simmer for 10 minutes or until liquid is reduced by one-third. Add reserved vegetables and seafood to sauce and cook for 1-2 minutes or until heated through. Season to taste with black pepper and serve immediately.

GOAN FISH CURRY
Serves 6

750 g/1¹/₂ lb boneless fish fillets, cut
into 5 cm/2 in strips
1 tblspn lime juice
1 tspn ground turmeric
60 g/2 oz ghee or butter
1 onion, chopped
1 tblspn Vindaloo curry paste
1 tblspn tamarind paste dissolved in
3 tblspn hot water
1¹/₂ cups/375 mL/12 fl oz coconut milk
1 green pepper, chopped

1 Place fish in a shallow glass or ceramic dish, sprinkle with lime juice and turmeric and toss to combine. Cover and marinate at room temperature for 2 hours.

2 Melt ghee or butter in a saucepan over a medium heat, add onion and cook, stirring, for 5 minutes or until onion is golden. Stir in curry paste and cook, stirring, for 10 minutes longer or until fragrant. Add tamarind mixture and coconut milk, bring to simmering and simmer, stirring occasionally, for 10 minutes.

3 Add fish and simmer for 10 minutes, then stir in green pepper.

FRIED FISH WITH CURRY SAUCE
Serves 2

1 tspn sea salt
3 cloves garlic, chopped
freshly ground black pepper
2 x 315 g/10 oz whole fish such as bream,
sea perch or snapper, cleaned and skin scored
¹/₄ cup/30 g/1 oz cornflour
vegetable oil for deep-frying

CURRY SAUCE
1 tblspn vegetable oil
2 small fresh red chillies, cut into thin strips
3 spring onions, sliced diagonally
2 tspn Thai red curry paste
1 tspn honey
³/₄ cup/185 mL/6 fl oz coconut milk
1 tblspn finely grated lime rind
1 tblspn lime juice

1 Combine salt, garlic and black pepper and rub over fish. Toss fish in cornflour and shake off excess.

2 Heat oil in a wok over a high heat, add fish and cook for 5 minutes on each side or until flesh flakes when tested with a fork. Drain on absorbent kitchen paper and keep warm.

3 Sauce: Heat oil in a wok or frying pan over a medium heat, add chillies and spring onions and stir-fry for 2 minutes. Add curry paste and stir-fry for 3 minutes longer or until fragrant. Stir in honey, coconut milk, lime rind and lime juice and bring to simmering. Simmer, stirring frequently, for 10 minutes. Serve with fish.

FRIED RICE
Serves 4-6

1 tblspn sesame oil
4 rashers bacon, chopped
1 clove garlic, crushed
1 tblspn finely grated fresh ginger
1 red pepper, chopped
1 carrot, cut into thin strips
250 g/8 oz uncooked prawns,
shelled and deveined, tails left intact
2 cups/440 g/14 oz long grain rice,
cooked and cooled
60 g/2 oz frozen peas
4 spring onions, sliced diagonally
1 tblspn soy sauce

CHINESE OMELETTE
1 tblspn vegetable oil
2 eggs, lightly beaten

1 Omelette: Heat oil in a frying pan over a medium heat. Pour in eggs, swirl to coat base of pan and cook for 3 minutes or until set. Cool, then roll up and cut into strips.

2 Heat sesame oil in a wok over a medium heat, add bacon, garlic and ginger and stir-fry until brown. Drain mixture on absorbent kitchen paper.

3 Add red pepper and carrot to wok and stir-fry for 3 minutes. Add prawns and stir-fry for 5 minutes. Add rice, omelette strips, bacon mixture, peas, spring onions and soy sauce and stir-fry for 5 minutes or until peas are cooked and mixture is heated through.

SALMON WITH HERB MASCARPONE
Serves 4

1 tblspn olive oil
$^1/_4$ cup/60 mL/2 fl oz lime juice
1 tspn ground cumin
$^1/_2$ tspn chilli powder
750 g/1$^1/_2$ lb salmon fillet, cut into 4 pieces
assorted lettuce leaves
balsamic or red wine vinegar

HERBED MASCARPONE
185 g/6 oz mascarpone
2 tblspn chopped fresh chives
1 tblspn chopped fresh dill
1 tblspn chopped fresh chervil
freshly ground black pepper

1 Combine oil, lime juice, cumin and chilli powder and brush over salmon. Reserve remaining oil mixture.

2 Heat a char-grill or frying pan over a high heat, add salmon and cook, brushing with remaining oil mixture, for 1-2 minutes each side or until flesh flakes when tested with a fork.

3 Herbed Mascarpone: Combine mascarpone, chives, dill, chervil and black pepper to taste.

4 Arrange lettuce leaves on serving plates and sprinkle with vinegar. Top with salmon and a spoonful of Herbed Mascarpone.

april
avril
april
abril

1	8	15
2	9	16
3	10	17
4	11	18
5	12	19
6	13	20
7	14	21

22	29
23	30
24	
25	
26	
27	
28	

MEATY MATTERS

Lean meat is an important part of a balanced diet. A 125 g/4 oz serving of cooked lean beef, lamb or pork provides much of the daily requirements of protein, the B-group vitamins, iron and zinc.

The more cutting and preparation meat has had, the shorter the storage time; for example, mince has a shorter storage time than chops or steak.

When shaping minced meat mixtures, dampen your hands and work on a lightly floured or dampened surface – this prevents the mince from sticking to your hands and the work surface.

If a casserole or stew is accidentally oversalted, add three or four thick slices of potato and cook until the excess salt is absorbed. Discard potato slices before serving.

Reduce fat intake by cutting all visible fat from meat before cooking.

LAMB AND SPINACH PIZZA
Serves 6

1 cup/185 g/6 oz burghul (cracked wheat)
2 cups/500 mL/16 fl oz hot water
2 tspn olive oil
1 onion, chopped
1 clove garlic, crushed
500 g/1 lb lean lamb mince
¹/₂ tspn dried mixed herbs
1 tblspn lemon juice
1 tblspn chopped fresh mint
¹/₂ tspn chilli powder

HUMMUS TOPPING
³/₄ cup/220 g/7 oz ready-made hummus
2 tomatoes, sliced
8 spinach leaves, blanched and chopped
3 tblspn pine nuts
4 tblspn grated mature Cheddar cheese

1 Soak burghul (cracked wheat) in water for 10-15 minutes.

2 Heat oil in a frying pan over a medium heat, add onion and garlic and cook, stirring, for 3-4 minutes. Drain burghul (cracked wheat), add onion mixture, lamb, mixed herbs, lemon juice, mint and chilli powder and mix to combine. Press lamb mixture into a 30 cm/12 in pizza tray and bake at 180°C/350°F/Gas 4 for 20 minutes or until firm. Drain off any juices.

3 Topping: Spread hummus over lamb pizza base then top with tomato slices and spinach. Sprinkle with pine nuts and cheese and cook under a preheated medium grill for 3-5 minutes or until cheese melts.

FIERY LAMB AND POTATO CURRY
Serves 4

1 onion, roughly chopped
2 cloves garlic, chopped
2.5 cm/1 in piece fresh ginger, roughly chopped
30 g/1 oz ghee or butter
2 tblspn Madras curry paste
500 g/1 lb lamb chops, trimmed of all visible fat
6 small new potatoes, halved
90 g/3 oz sultanas
$1^1/2$ cups/375 mL/12 fl oz coconut milk
2 tblspn chopped fresh mint
1 cinnamon stick

1 Place onion, garlic and ginger into a food processor or blender and process to finely chop.

2 Melt ghee or butter in a large nonstick frying pan over a medium heat, add onion mixture and cook, stirring, for 2 minutes or until mixture is golden. Stir in curry paste and cook for 2 minutes longer or until fragrant.

3 Add chops and cook for 5 minutes each side or until brown. Add potatoes, sultanas, coconut milk, mint and cinnamon, bring to simmering and simmer, stirring occasionally, for 40 minutes or until meat is tender.

33

NAVARIN LAMB
Serves 6

6 lamb noisettes or loin chops
1 onion, sliced
1 clove garlic, crushed
1 tspn chopped fresh rosemary or
$^1/_2$ tspn dried rosemary
440 g/14 oz canned tomatoes,
undrained and mashed
1 cup/250 mL/8 fl oz chicken stock
$^1/_2$ cup/125 mL/4 fl oz dry red wine
12 small new potatoes
12 pickling onions or shallots
6 small carrots, scrubbed
250 g/8 oz green beans, cut into
5 cm/2 in pieces
freshly ground black pepper

1 Heat a nonstick frying pan over a medium heat, add lamb and cook for 3-4 minutes each side or until brown. Remove lamb from pan and place in a casserole dish.

2 Add sliced onion, garlic, rosemary and 1 tblspn juice from tomatoes to pan and cook, stirring, for 5 minutes or until onion is soft. Stir tomatoes, stock and wine into pan, bring to the boil, then reduce heat and simmer for 15 minutes or until mixture reduces and thickens. Add sauce to casserole, cover and bake at 180°C/350°F/Gas 4 for 1 hour. Add potatoes and onions or shallots and bake for 1 hour longer or until meat and vegetables are tender.

3 Boil or microwave carrots and beans separately until just tender, drain and refresh under cold running water. Add carrots and beans to casserole and bake for 20 minutes longer. Season with black pepper.

ROAST LAMB AND VEGETABLES
Serves 6

1.5 kg/3 lb leg lamb
2 cloves garlic, peeled and thinly sliced
1 sprig fresh rosemary
$^{1}/_{2}$ cup/125 mL/4 fl oz water

ROAST VEGETABLES
6 potatoes, peeled and halved
6 small onions, peeled
500 g/1 lb pumpkin, peeled and cut into wedges
or 2 large sweet potatoes, peeled and cut into
large pieces or 3 parsnips, peeled and
halved lengthwise
2 tblspn vegetable oil

1 Cut several deep slits in the surface of the lamb. Fill each slit with a slice of garlic and 1-2 rosemary leaves. Place lamb on a roasting rack in a roasting tin. Pour water into roasting tin and bake at 190°C/375°F/Gas 5 for 1$^{1}/_{4}$ hours or until cooked to your liking. Place lamb on a warm serving platter, cover and rest for 10 minutes before serving.

2 Roast Vegetables: Place potatoes, onions and pumpkin, sweet potatoes or parsnips around meat or in a greased baking dish. Brush with oil and bake, turning occasionally, for 1 hour or until tender.

may
mai mai
mayo

1	8	15
2	9	16
3	10	17
4	11	18
5	12	19
6	13	20
7	14	21

22	29
23	30
24	31
25	
26	
27	
28	

SAFE BARBECUING

Check the barbecue area before lighting the barbecue. Do not have the barbecue too close to the house and sweep up any dry leaves or anything that might catch fire if hit by a spark.

Watch a lighted barbecue at all times. Keep children and pets away from hot barbecues and equipment.

Do not barbecue in enclosed areas. If wet weather has forced you to move your barbecue under cover, ensure there is plenty of ventilation.

If you have a gas barbecue, before lighting it check that all the gas fittings and hose connections are tight.

If your gas barbecue does not light the first time, turn it off, wait 20 seconds and try again. This will ensure that there is not a gas build-up.

Always turn a gas barbecue off at the gas bottle as well as at the controls.

CAJUN BARBECUE
Serves 4

4 cobs sweet corn, halved
1 orange sweet potato, cut into
1 cm/^{1}/$_2$ in thick slices
30 g/1 oz butter, melted
4 rump or sirloin steaks
CAJUN SPICE MIX
1 tspn freshly ground black pepper
^{1}/$_2$ tspn chilli powder
1 tspn ground cumin
1 tspn ground coriander
2 tspn sweet paprika

1 Spice Mix: Combine black pepper, chilli powder, cumin, coriander and paprika.

2 Brush sweet corn and sweet potato with butter. Then sprinkle spice mix over vegetables and steaks. Cook corn and sweet potato on a preheated hot barbecue, turning frequently, for 10-15 minutes or until almost cooked. Add steaks and cook for 3-5 minutes each side or until cooked to your liking.

BEEF AND BACON BURGERS
Serves 6

750 g/1¹/₂ lb lean beef mince
3 spring onions, chopped
2 tblspn snipped fresh chives
1 egg, lightly beaten
2 tblspn tomato sauce
1 tblspn Worcestershire sauce
1 tblspn chilli sauce
125 g/4 oz grated mozzarella cheese
6 rashers bacon, rind removed

1 Combine beef, spring onions, chives, egg, tomato sauce, Worcestershire sauce and chilli sauce. Shape mixture into twelve patties. Top six patties with mozzarella cheese, then with remaining patties and pinch edges together to seal. Wrap a rasher of bacon around each pattie and secure with a wooden toothpick or cocktail stick. Chill for 2 hours or until firm.

2 Cook patties on a preheated medium barbecue grill for 5-7 minutes each side or until cooked to your liking and cheese melts.

BEEF AND BEAN STIR-FRY
Serves 4

250 g/8 oz quick-cooking noodles
2 tspn sesame oil
2 cloves garlic, crushed
3 tspn finely grated fresh ginger
500 g/1 lb rump steak, cut into thin strips
500 g/1 lb snake or green beans, trimmed
and cut into 10 cm/4 in pieces
2 tblspn sweet chilli sauce
2 tblspn sweet soy sauce
1 tblspn oyster sauce

1 Prepare noodles following packet directions.

2 Heat oil in a wok or frying pan over a medium heat, add garlic and ginger and stir-fry for 1 minute. Add beef and stir-fry for 3 minutes or until well browned. Add beans, chilli sauce, soy sauce and oyster sauce and stir-fry for 2 minutes longer.

3 Drain noodles and divide between serving plates. Top with beef mixture and serve immediately.

GINGER BEEF WITH CASHEWS
Serves 4

500 g/1 lb lean beef
1 tblspn vegetable oil
2 cloves garlic, crushed
1 tspn finely grated fresh ginger
$^1/_2$ Chinese cabbage (pak choi), shredded
$^1/_2$ red pepper, sliced thinly
30 g/1 oz bean sprouts
$1^1/_2$ tblspn soy sauce
3 x 75 g/$2^1/_2$ oz packets quick-cooking noodles,
cooked and kept warm
60 g/2 oz raw cashews, roasted

1 Slice beef thinly across the grain. Heat oil in a wok over a medium heat, add garlic and ginger and stir-fry for 1 minute. Increase heat to high, add beef and stir-fry for 2-3 minutes or until meat is brown.

2 Add cabbage, red pepper, bean sprouts and soy sauce and stir-fry for 2 minutes or until cabbage just starts to wilt. Divide noodles between serving plates, top with beef mixture and scatter with cashews.

CHILLI CON CARNE
Serves 4

1 tblspn olive oil
1 onion, finely chopped
2 cloves garlic, crushed
1 green pepper, chopped
500 g/1 lb lean beef mince
2 tspn ground paprika
$^1/_2$ tspn chilli powder
$^1/_2$ tspn ground cumin
1 tspn minced red chilli
440 g/14 oz canned tomato purée (passata)
$^1/_2$ cup/125 mL/4 fl oz beef stock
$^1/_2$ cup/125 mL/4 fl oz red wine
315 g/10 oz canned red kidney beans,
drained and rinsed
freshly ground black pepper
vegetable oil for deep-frying
4 tortillas
$^1/_2$ cup/125 g/4 oz sour cream

1 Heat olive oil in a frying pan over a medium heat, add onion, garlic and green pepper and cook stirring, for 3-4 minutes. Stir in beef and cook for 5 minutes or until brown.

2 Add paprika, chilli powder, cumin, chilli, tomato purée (passata), stock and wine, bring to simmering and simmer, stirring occasionally, for 25 minutes or until liquid is reduced by half. Stir in beans and black pepper to taste and cook for 10 minutes longer.

3 Heat vegetable oil in a large saucepan until a cube of bread dropped in browns in 50 seconds. Cook tortillas one at a time, pushing down with a small ladle, to make a basket shape, for 3-4 minutes or until golden. Drain. Spoon meat mixture into tortilla baskets and top with sour cream.

MEDITERRANEAN FRITTATA
Serves 6

1 tblspn olive oil
1 red onion, sliced
250 g/8 oz lean beef mince
2 slices pancetta or bacon, cut into strips
2 cloves garlic, crushed
2 tblspn finely chopped fresh basil
60 g/2 oz sun-dried tomatoes, sliced
60 g/2 oz black olives, chopped
2 potatoes, cooked and sliced
6 eggs, lightly beaten
60 g/2 oz grated fresh Parmesan cheese
freshly ground black pepper

1 Heat oil in a large frying pan over a medium heat, add onion and cook, stirring, for 3-4 minutes or until onion is soft. Remove onion from pan and set aside. Add beef, pancetta or bacon and garlic to pan and cook, stirring, for 5 minutes or until meat is brown. Drain off cooking juices.

2 Stir basil, sun-dried tomatoes and olives into meat mixture and spoon into a greased 20 cm/8 in pie dish. Top with onions and potatoes.

3 Place eggs, Parmesan cheese and black pepper to taste in a bowl and whisk to combine. Pour egg mixture into pie dish and bake at 180°C/350°F/ Gas 4 for 20-25 minutes or until frittata is set.

june juin juni junio

1	8	15
2	9	16
3	10	17
4	11	18
5	12	19
6	13	20
7	14	21

22	29
23	30
24	
25	
26	
27	
28	

KEEPING IT SAFE

Do not handle cooked and uncooked meat, poultry or fish at the same time. This encourages the transfer of bacteria.

Wash thoroughly in hot soapy water utensils and boards that have been used for cutting raw meat, before using them to cut cooked meat.

Thoroughly wash your hands after preparing raw meat.

Storing raw meat, poultry or fish above or in direct contact with cooked foods can lead to the raw food dripping liquid or passing bacteria to the cooked food.

Food that has been prepared in advance must be kept chilled until just prior to cooking.

Store cold foods at temperatures below 4°C/39°F and keep hot food at temperatures above 60°C/140°F. Foods held at temperatures between these two are more likely to develop bacteria which can cause food poisoning.

FRIED PORKBALLS
Makes 24

500 g/1 lb lean pork mince
30 g/1 oz rice noodles, broken, soaked
and well-soaked
1 small onion, finely chopped
1 clove garlic, crushed
1 tspn finely grated fresh ginger
1 tspn finely chopped fresh lemon grass or
1 tspn finely grated lemon rind
1/4 tspn ground turmeric
freshly ground black pepper
flour
vegetable oil for deep-frying

1 Combine pork and noodles. Place onion, garlic ginger and lemon grass or lemon rind in a food processor and process to make a paste. Add onion mixture, turmeric and black pepper to taste to pork mixture and mix to combine.

2 Form pork mixture into 24 balls, dust with flour place on a plate lined with plastic food wrap and refrigerate for 15 minutes or until required. Heat oil in a large saucepan until a cube of bread dropped in browns in 50 seconds. Cook porkballs a few at a time for 3-4 minutes or until golden and cooked through. Drain on absorbent kitchen paper and serve immediately.

COUNTRY TERRINE
Serves 10

750 g/1¹/₂ lb pork and veal mince
1 onion, finely chopped
2 cloves garlic, crushed
4 spinach leaves, shredded
10 pitted prunes, roughly chopped
1 large green apple, finely diced
60 g/2 oz pine nuts
¹/₄ cup/60 mL/2 fl oz brandy
¹/₄ cup/30 g/1 oz flour
¹/₂ cup/125 mL/4 fl oz cream (double)
2 tspn chopped fresh parsley
freshly ground black pepper
500 g/1 lb bacon rashers, rind removed

1 Combine mince, onion, garlic, spinach, prunes, apple, pine nuts, brandy, flour, cream, parsley and black pepper to taste.

2 Line a lightly greased 11 x 21 cm/4¹/₂ x 8¹/₂ in loaf tin with bacon rashers allowing them to overhang the top. Pack meat mixture into loaf tin and smooth top. Fold overhanging rashers to cover filling. Cover tin tightly with a double thickness of aluminium foil. Place in a baking dish with enough hot water to come halfway up sides of tin and bake at 180°C/350°F/Gas 4 for 1¹/₂ hours or until mixture is coming away from sides of tin and is cooked through. Remove foil, drain off excess liquid and refrigerate overnight.

HUNGARIAN PORK SLICE
Serves 4

$^1/_2$ large cabbage, leaves separated
1 tblspn vegetable oil
1 onion, chopped
2 cloves garlic, crushed
500 g/1 lb lean pork mince
$^1/_3$ cup/75 g/2$^1/_2$ oz short grain rice, cooked
$^3/_4$ cup/45 g/1$^1/_2$ oz breadcrumbs,
made from stale bread
$^1/_2$ cup/125 mL/4 fl oz milk
$^1/_2$ tspn dried marjoram
$^1/_4$ tspn caraway seeds
1 tblspn ground paprika
2 eggs, lightly beaten
freshly ground black pepper
4 rashers bacon, rind removed

1 Boil or microwave cabbage leaves until tender. Drain, refresh under cold water and drain again. Line a greased, shallow 20 cm/8 in round ovenproof dish with some of the cabbage leaves. Set remaining leaves aside.

2 Heat oil in a frying pan, add onion and garlic and cook until onion is soft. Cool. Combine pork, rice, breadcrumbs, milk, marjoram, caraway seeds, paprika, eggs, black pepper to taste and onion mixture.

3 Spoon half the pork mixture into cabbage-lined dish, top with a layer of cabbage leaves and the remaining pork mixture. Arrange bacon over top, cover and bake at 180°C/350°F/Gas 4 for 1 hour or until cooked. Drain off cooking juices and reserve.

4 To serve, invert slice onto a serving plate, cut into wedges.

PORK WITH VINEGAR AND HERBS
Serves 4

1 tblspn chopped fresh thyme or
1 tspn dried thyme
1 tblspn chopped fresh sage or
1 tspn dried sage
1 tblspn vegetable oil
4 pork loin chops, trimmed of all visible fat
$^1/_2$ cup/125 mL/4 fl oz red wine vinegar
freshly ground black pepper
2 tblspn chopped fresh parsley or basil

1 Place thyme, sage and oil in a shallow glass or ceramic dish and mix to combine. Add chops and turn to coat. Cover and marinate for 1 hour.

2 Heat a nonstick frying pan over a medium heat, add chops and cook for 3-4 minutes each side or until brown. Stir in vinegar, reduce heat and simmer for 25-30 minutes or until pork is tender and vinegar reduced. Season to taste with black pepper and sprinkle with parsley or basil.

july
juillet juli
julio

1	8	15
2	9	16
3	10	17
4	11	18
5	12	19
6	13	20
7	14	21

22	29
23	30
24	31
25	
26	
27	
28	

PERFECT POTATOES

Potato Wedges: Cut small potatoes into wedges and boil or microwave until tender. Drain and pat dry. Toss potatoes with $1/4$ teaspoon chilli powder, 1 teaspoon ground turmeric, $1/2$ teaspoon garam masala, 1 teaspoon ground coriander and $1/2$ teaspoon ground ginger to coat. Shallow-fry for 5-10 minutes until potatoes are crisp.

Potato Crisps: Using a vegetable peeler, peel thin slices from potatoes. Dry slices and deep-fry for 7-10 minutes or until cooked. Drain and sprinkle with salt.

Potato Salad: Boil or microwave potatoes in their skins until tender. Drain, rinse under cold running water and set aside to cool. Cut potatoes into pieces – there is no need to peel. Place potatoes in a salad bowl with snipped chives, chopped parsley and chopped red or green pepper. Top with mayonnaise and toss to combine.

CHICKEN AND PENNE SALAD
Serves 4

500 g/1 lb penne, cooked and cooled
1 kg/2 lb cooked chicken, skin removed
and flesh shredded
1 green pepper, chopped
3 tblspn snipped fresh chives
440 g/14 oz canned sweet corn kernels, drained
2 stalks celery, chopped
250 g/8 oz yellow teardrop or red
cherry tomatoes
250 g/8 oz curly endive
³/4 cup/185 mL/6 fl oz creamy salad dressing

Arrange penne, chicken, green pepper, chives sweet corn, celery, tomatoes and endive on a large serving platter or in a large salad bowl. Spoon dressing over and serve immediately.

CHICKEN IN APPLE CIDER
Serves 4

1 tblspn olive oil
2 cloves garlic, crushed
10 pickling onions or shallots
4 boneless chicken breast fillets
3 tblspn fresh tarragon leaves or
1 tblspn dried tarragon
1 cup/250 mL/8 fl oz apple cider
1 cup/250 mL/8 fl oz chicken stock
$^1/_4$ cup/60 mL/2 fl oz dry white wine
1 tblspn tarragon or white wine vinegar
1 cup/200 g/6$^1/_2$ oz low-fat natural yogurt
freshly ground black pepper

1 Heat oil in a large frying pan over a medium heat, add garlic and onions or shallots and cook, stirring, for 5 minutes. Add chicken and cook, turning, for 10 minutes or until golden on all sides.

2 Add tarragon, cider, stock, wine and vinegar to pan and bring to the boil. Reduce heat, cover and simmer for 30 minutes or until chicken is tender. Remove pan from heat, stir in yogurt and season to taste with black pepper.

CHICKEN CASSOULET
Serves 6

750 g/1¹/2 lb dried haricot or
borlotti beans
2 tblspn olive oil
1 kg/2 lb chicken thigh or breast fillets,
cut into 2 cm/³/4 in cubes
2 cloves garlic, thinly sliced
2 onions, chopped
2 leeks, sliced
250 g/8 oz salami, chopped
2 x 440 g/14 oz canned tomatoes,
undrained and mashed
¹/2 cup/125 mL/4 fl oz dry white wine
1 bouquet garni
freshly ground black pepper
2 cups/125 g/4 oz wholemeal breadcrumbs,
made from stale bread

1 Place beans in a large bowl, cover with water and set aside to soak overnight, then drain. Place beans in a large saucepan with enough water to cover and bring to the boil. Boil for 10 minutes then reduce heat and simmer for 1 hour or until beans are tender. Drain and set aside.

2 Heat oil in a large saucepan over a medium heat add chicken and cook, stirring for 10 minutes or until chicken is brown on all sides. Remove from pan and drain on absorbent kitchen paper.

3 Add garlic, onions and leeks to pan and cook stirring, for 5 minutes or until onions are golden Add salami, tomatoes, wine and bouquet garni and bring to the boil. Reduce heat and simmer for 10 minutes. Return chicken to pan, cover and simmer for 30 minutes or until chicken is tender Season to taste with black pepper.

4 Spoon half the chicken mixture into a large casserole dish and top with half the beans. Repeat with remaining chicken mixture and beans to use all ingredients. Sprinkle with breadcrumbs and bake at 200°C/400°F/Gas 6, uncovered, for 30 minutes or until hot and bubbling and top is golden.

CHICKEN POT PIE
Serves 4

60 g/2 oz butter
1 large onion, chopped
4 chicken breast fillets, cut into 2 cm/^{3}/4 in cubes
2 potatoes, cut into 1 cm/^{1}/2 in cubes
2 large carrots, cut into 1 cm/^{1}/2 in cubes
^{1}/4 cup/30 g/1 oz flour
1 cup/250 mL/8 fl oz dry white wine
3 cups/750 mL/1^1/4 pt chicken stock
1 cup/250 mL/8 fl oz cream (double)
2 tblspn tomato paste (purée)

HERBED SCONE TOPPING
2 cups/250 g/8 oz self-raising flour, sifted
1 tspn dried mixed herbs
30 g/1 oz grated fresh Parmesan cheese
30 g/1 oz butter, chopped
1 cup/250 mL/8 fl oz milk

1 Melt butter in a frying pan over a medium heat, add onion, stirring, over a medium heat for 3-4 minutes. Add chicken and cook, stirring, for 3 minutes longer.

2 Add potatoes and carrots and cook, stirring, for 8-10 minutes. Stir in flour, then wine, stock, cream and tomato paste (purée), and bring to simmering. Simmer for 10 minutes then transfer mixture to a casserole dish.

3 Topping: Combine flour, mixed herbs, Parmesan cheese and butter in a food processor. With machine running, add milk and process to form a sticky dough. Knead dough on a floured surface until smooth. Press dough out to 2 cm/^{3}/4 in thick and cut out rounds. Place on top of casserole.

4 Bake at 200°C/400°F/Gas 6 for 20-25 minutes or until topping is cooked and casserole is hot.

CHICKEN ROLL CASSEROLE
Serves 6

6 boneless chicken breast fillets, skin removed
3 rashers bacon, rind removed
1 tblspn chopped fresh parsley
60 g/2 oz butter
2 onions, chopped
2 carrots, grated
8 spinach leaves
freshly ground black pepper
3 potatoes, cooked and sliced
^{1}/2 cup/125 mL/4 fl oz water

1 Place fillets between two sheets of plastic food wrap and pound, using a rolling pin, to flatten. Cut bacon rashers in half. Place a piece of bacon on each chicken fillet and sprinkle with parsley.

Fold the shorter ends of the fillets into the centre, then roll up and secure with toothpicks.

2 Melt half the butter in a large frying pan and cook chicken rolls for 8-10 minutes or until brown on all sides. Remove rolls from pan and set aside.

3 Melt remaining butter in frying pan and cook onions and carrots, stirring, for 5 minutes or until onions are soft. Add spinach and cook, stirring, for 2-3 minutes longer or until spinach is wilted. Season to taste with black pepper.

4 Place potatoes in the base of a casserole dish. Top with vegetable mixture, then chicken rolls. Pour water over, cover and bake at 180°C/350°F/ Gas 4 for 35-40 minutes or until rolls are cooked.

TANDOORI CHICKEN POCKETS
Serves 6

3 tblspn Tandoori curry paste
1^1/$_4$ cups/250 g/8 oz natural yogurt
12 boneless chicken thigh fillets or 6 boneless
chicken breast fillets
6 wholemeal pitta bread rounds

MANGO RELISH
2 mangoes, seeded, peeled and chopped
2 tomatoes, chopped
1 tblspn finely chopped fresh mint
1 red onion, finely chopped
1 tblspn vinegar

1 Combine curry paste and yogurt in a bowl. Add chicken and toss to coat. Marinate in the refrigerator overnight.

2 Drain chicken and cook on a lightly oiled preheated medium barbecue or under a grill for 15 minutes or until chicken is tender. Make a slit in the top of each pitta bread round. Cut chicken in to thick slices and divide between pockets.

3 Relish: Combine mangoes, tomatoes, mint onion and vinegar and spoon into pockets. Serve immediately.

COCONUT CHICKEN CURRY
Serves 4

1 tblspn vegetable oil
1 onion, chopped
1 clove garlic, crushed
1 tblspn finely grated fresh ginger
1 tblspn green curry paste
1^1/$_2$ cups/375 mL/12 fl oz coconut milk
1 tblspn Thai fish sauce
1 tblspn brown sugar
1 tblspn finely grated lemon rind
4 boneless chicken breast fillets, sliced
1 tblspn chopped fresh basil
1 tblspn chopped fresh mint
440 g/14 oz canned baby sweet corn, drained
220 g/7 oz canned bamboo shoots, drained
3 zucchini (courgettes), sliced
125 g/4 oz frozen peas

1 Heat oil in a saucepan over a medium heat, add onion, garlic and ginger and stir-fry for 3 minutes. Stir in curry paste and cook for 3 minutes longer or until fragrant.

2 Stir in coconut milk, fish sauce, sugar and lemon rind. Bring to simmering and simmer for 10 minutes. Add chicken, basil and mint and simmer for 10 minutes or until chicken is tender.

3 Add sweet corn, bamboo shoots, zucchini (courgettes) and peas and cook for 5 minutes or until peas are tender.

august
août

august
agosto

1	8	15
2	9	16
3	10	17
4	11	18
5	12	19
6	13	20
7	14	21

22	29
23	30
24	31
25	
26	
27	
28	

PASTA

For perfect results when cooking pasta, allow approximately 4 litres/7 pt of water to 500 g/1 lb pasta and use a very large saucepan. Bring the water to a rapid boil, add a dash of oil and a pinch of salt. The oil prevents the pasta from sticking and the salt helps bring out the flavour. Add the pasta, give a stir and cook for the required time.

Pasta is cooked when it is 'al dente' (to the tooth tender but some resistance to the bite). It should not be overcooked and mushy.

Cooking times vary, depending on the type of pasta. Commercially packaged, dried pasta takes 10-12 minutes to cook, while fresh pasta takes 3-5 minutes. Once the pasta is cooked, drain and toss with a little oil or melted butter to prevent the pasta sticking.

The only time you should rinse cooked pasta under cold water is when you are using it in a salad. This prevents if from sticking together.

SPICY AVOCADO AND CHILLI PASTA
Serves 4

500 g/1 lb spaghetti
4 tblspn sour cream or natural yogurt
250 g/8 oz corn chips
SPICY AVOCADO SAUCE
1 avocado, stoned, peeled and chopped
3 ripe tomatoes, chopped
$^{1}/_{2}$ green pepper, chopped
1 fresh red chilli, chopped
2 tspn finely grated lime rind
1 tblspn lime juice
2 tblspn balsamic or red wine vinegar

1 Cook pasta in boiling water in a large saucepan following packet directions, drain, set aside and keep warm.

2 Sauce: Combine avocado, tomatoes, green pepper, chilli, lime rind, lime juice and vinegar.

3 Add sauce to pasta and toss to combine. Serve topped with sour cream or yogurt and corn chips on the side.

PASTA WITH ROASTED GARLIC AND TOMATOES
Serves 8

2 tblspn olive oil
16 plum (egg or Italian) tomatoes, quartered
32 cloves garlic, unpeeled
sea salt
500 g/1 lb fresh fettuccine
MINT PESTO
125 g/4 oz fresh mint
4 tblspn grated Parmesan cheese
1 clove garlic, crushed
3 tblspn pine nuts
3 tblspn olive oil

1 Place oil, tomatoes and garlic in a baking dish. Toss to coat and sprinkle with sea salt. Bake at 180°C/350°F/Gas 4 for 35 minutes or until garlic is golden. Keep warm.

2 Pesto: Place mint leaves, Parmesan cheese, garlic and pine nuts in a food processor and process until finely chopped. With machine running, gradually add oil and continue processing to make a thick paste.

3 Cook pasta in boiling water in a large saucepan following packet directions. Drain and keep warm. Remove skin from garlic cloves. Divide hot pasta between serving plates, top with roasted tomatoes, garlic and pesto.

LINGUINE WITH CHILLI AND LEMON
Serves 4

500 g/1 lb fresh linguine or spaghetti
2 tblspn olive oil
6 cloves garlic, peeled
2 fresh red chillies, seeded and sliced
125 g/4 oz rocket, leaves removed and shredded
3 tspn finely grated lemon rind
2 tblspn lemon juice
freshly ground black pepper
90 g/3 oz grated fresh Parmesan cheese

1 Cook pasta in boiling water in a large saucepan, following packet directions. Drain, set aside and keep warm.

2 Heat oil in a frying pan over a low heat, add garlic and chillies and cook, stirring, for 6 minutes or until garlic is golden. Add garlic mixture, rocket, lemon rind, lemon juice, black pepper to taste and Parmesan cheese to hot pasta and toss to combine.

SPAGHETTI MARINARA
Serves 4

500 g/1 lb spaghetti
2 tspn vegetable oil
2 onions, chopped
2 x 440 g/14 oz canned tomatoes,
undrained and mashed
2 tblspn chopped fresh basil or
1 tspn dried basil
1/4 cup/60 mL/2 fl oz dry white wine
12 mussels, scrubbed and
beards removed
12 scallops
12 uncooked prawns, shelled
and deveined
125 g/4 oz calamari (squid) rings

1 Cook pasta in boiling water in a large saucepan following packet directions. Drain, set aside and keep warm.

2 Heat oil and butter in a frying pan over a medium heat. Add onions and cook, stirring, for 4 minutes or until onions are golden.

3 Stir in tomatoes, basil and wine, bring to simmering and simmer for 8 minutes. Add mussels and cook for 3-4 minutes. Add scallops and prawns and cook for 2 minutes longer.

4 Add calamari (squid) and cook for 1 minute or until shellfish is cooked. Discard any unopened mussels. Spoon seafood mixture over hot pasta and serve.

FETTUCCINE ALFREDO
Serves 4

500 g/1 lb fettuccine
155 g/5 oz butter, softened and chopped
125 g/4 oz grated fresh Parmesan cheese
freshly ground black pepper

1 Cook pasta in boiling water in a large saucepan following packet directions. Drain well and place in a large serving bowl.

2 Scatter butter and Parmesan cheese over hot pasta, season to taste with black pepper, toss and serve immediately.

PASTA SALAD WITH ROASTED GARLIC
Serves 8

20 cloves unpeeled garlic
8 rashers bacon, chopped
30 g/1 oz butter
2 cups/125 g/4 oz breadcrumbs,
made from stale bread
4 tblspn chopped fresh mixed herb leaves
freshly ground black pepper
750 g/1^{1}/$_2$ lb spinach, tomato or
plain linguine

1 Place unpeeled garlic cloves on a lightly greased baking tray and bake at 180°C/350°F/Gas 4 for 10-12 minutes or until soft and golden. Peel garlic and set aside.

2 Cook bacon in a frying pan over a medium heat for 4-5 minutes or until crisp. Drain on absorbent kitchen paper.

3 Melt butter in a clean frying pan, add breadcrumbs, mixed herbs and black pepper to taste and cook, stirring, for 4-5 minutes or until breadcrumbs are golden.

4 Cook pasta in boiling water in a large saucepan following packet directions. Drain well and place in a warm serving bowl. Add garlic, bacon and breadcrumb mixture, toss and serve immediately.

SPICY BUCKWHEAT NOODLES
Serves 4

500 g/1 lb buckwheat noodles
1 tblspn olive oil
3 cloves garlic, crushed
2 fresh red chillies, seeded and chopped
200 g/6¹/₂ oz rocket, leaves removed
and shredded
2 tomatoes, chopped

1 Cook noodles in boiling water in a large saucepan following packet directions. Drain, set aside and keep warm.

2 Heat oil in a frying pan over a medium heat, add garlic and cook, stirring, for 1 minute. Add chillies, rocket and tomatoes and cook for 2 minutes or until rocket wilts. Toss vegetable mixture with noodles and serve immediately.

PENNE WITH GORGONZOLA SAUCE
Serves 4

500 g/1 lb penne

GORGONZOLA SAUCE
1 cup/250 mL/8 fl oz cream (double)
$^1/_2$ cup/125 mL/4 fl oz vegetable stock
$^1/_2$ cup/125 mL/4 fl oz white wine
125 g/4 oz Gorgonzola or
blue cheese, crumbled
2 tblspn chopped flat-leaf parsley
$^1/_2$ tspn ground nutmeg
freshly ground black pepper

1 Cook pasta in boiling water in a large saucepan following packet directions. Drain, set aside and keep warm.

2 Sauce: Place cream, stock, wine and Gorgonzola or blue cheese in a saucepan and cook, over a medium heat, stirring constantly, until smooth. Bring to simmering and simmer for 8 minutes or until sauce thickens.

3 Add parsley, nutmeg and black pepper to taste, bring to simmering and simmer for 2 minutes. Spoon sauce over hot pasta and serve.

1	8	15
2	9	16
3	10	17
4	11	18
5	12	19
6	13	20
7	14	21

22	29
23	30
24	
25	
26	
27	
28	

MAKING THE MOST
OF VEGETABLES

Wash vegetables before preparing, but do not soak. Soaking tends to draw out the valuable water-soluble vitamins thereby decreasing the nutrient content. However it may be necessary to soak very dirty vegetables to remove dirt and creepy-crawlies. If this is the case, keep soaking times to a minimum.

Vegetables that are left whole with their skins on have a higher nutrient and fibre content than those that are finely chopped and peeled. Many of the precious vitamins and minerals found in vegetables are stored just under the skin. Only peel vegetables if necessary.

When handling fresh chillies do not put your hands near your eyes or allow them to touch your lips. To avoid discomfort and burning wear rubber gloves.

Recent studies have shown that the fibre in legumes is soluble, and when eaten as part of a low-fat diet, helps to lower blood cholestrol levels and control glucose levels in diabetics.

ITALIAN POTATO BAKE
Serves 4

6 potatoes, sliced
$^1/_2$ cup/125 g/4 oz ready-made pesto
2 yellow or green zucchini (courgettes),
sliced lengthwise
$^1/_2$ cup/125 g/4 oz olive paste (pâté)
6 baby eggplant (aubergines), sliced lengthwise
$^1/_2$ cup/125 mL/4 fl oz milk
$^1/_2$ cup/125 g/4 oz sour cream
60 g/2 oz grated fresh Parmesan cheese
freshly ground black pepper

1 Arrange one-third of the potatoes over the base of an ovenproof dish. Top with pesto, zucchini (courgettes) and half the remaining potatoes. Top potatoes with olive paste (pâté), eggplant (aubergines) and remaining potatoes.

2 Combine milk and sour cream and carefully pour over vegetables. Sprinkle with Parmesan cheese and black pepper to taste and bake at 200°C/400°F/ Gas 6 for 50 minutes or until potatoes are tender.

VEGETABLE RAGOUT
Serves 4

45 g/1¹/₂ oz butter
2 onions, chopped
2 cloves garlic, crushed
¹/₃ cup/45 g/1¹/₂ oz flour
2 cups/250 mL/8 fl oz milk
2 cups/500 mL/16 fl oz vegetable stock
2 parsnips, chopped
4 potatoes, chopped
250 g/8 oz button mushrooms
250 g/8 oz Brussels sprouts
2 zucchini (courgettes), chopped
2 tablespoons chopped fresh tarragon

1 Melt butter in a saucepan over a medium heat, add onions and garlic and cook, stirring, for 3 minutes or until soft. Stir in flour and cook for 2 minutes longer. Remove pan from heat and slowly stir in milk and stock, then cook, stirring constantly, until mixture boils and thickens.

2 Add parsnips and potatoes to sauce, bring to simmering and simmer for 10 minutes. Add mushrooms, Brussels sprouts, zucchini (courgettes) and tarragon and simmer for 10 minutes or until vegetables are tender.

STIR-FRY GREENS WITH SALSA
Serves 4

2 tspn olive oil
2 cloves garlic, crushed
250 g/8 oz asparagus spears, halved
250 g/8 oz green beans
12 spinach leaves
2 stalks celery, sliced
2 zucchini (courgettes), sliced
250 g/8 oz broccoli, cut into florets

RED PEPPER SALSA
1 tblspn vegetable oil
1 red pepper, chopped
1 ripe tomato, finely chopped
1/4 cup/60 mL/2 fl oz red wine
2 spring onions, chopped
freshly ground black pepper

1 Salsa: Heat oil in a frying pan over a medium heat, add red pepper and tomato and cook, stirring, until red pepper is soft. Add wine and cook, stirring, until wine is absorbed. Remove pan from heat and stir in spring onions and black pepper to taste. Set aside.

2 Heat olive oil in a clean frying pan over a medium heat, add garlic and stir-fry for 1 minute. Add asparagus, beans, spinach, celery, zucchini (courgettes) and broccoli and stir-fry for 5 minutes or until vegetables are tender but still crisp. Serve with salsa.

WARM ASPARAGUS SALAD
Serves 4

500 g/1 lb asparagus, trimmed
1 tspn Dijon mustard
1 tblspn red wine vinegar
3 tblspn olive oil
freshly ground black pepper

1 Boil, steam or microwave asparagus until just tender. Drain well.

2 Whisk together mustard, vinegar, oil and black pepper to taste. Spoon over warm asparagus and serve immediately.

SALAD NIÇOISE
Serves 4-6

1 lettuce of your choice, leaves separated
500 g/1 lb fresh young broad beans, shelled
1 large red pepper, cut into thin strips
8 marinated artichoke hearts, halved
250 g/8 oz cherry tomatoes
1 large cucumber, cut into strips
3 spring onions, chopped
12 canned anchovy fillets, drained
220 g/7 oz canned tuna in water, drained
185 g/6 oz marinated black olives

6 hard-boiled eggs, quartered
$^1/_4$ cup/60 mL/2 fl oz olive oil
freshly ground black pepper

Arrange lettuce leaves, beans, red pepper, artichokes, tomatoes, cucumber, spring onions, anchovy fillets, tuna, olives and eggs on a large serving platter or in a large salad bowl. Drizzle with oil and season to taste with black pepper.

POTATO GRATIN
Serves 6

1 kg/2 lb potatoes, thinly sliced
2 large onions, thinly sliced
2 tblspn snipped fresh chives
freshly ground black pepper
1¼ cups/250 g/8 oz low-fat natural yogurt
1 cup/250 mL/8 fl oz cream (double)
60 g/2 oz grated fresh Parmesan cheese

1 Layer potatoes, onions, chives and black pepper to taste in six lightly greased individual ovenproof dishes.

2 Place yogurt and cream in a bowl and mix to combine. Carefully pour yogurt mixture over potatoes and sprinkle with Parmesan cheese. Bake for 45 minutes or until potatoes are tender and top is golden.

october
octobre
oktober
octubre

1	8	15
2	9	16
3	10	17
4	11	18
5	12	19
6	13	20
7	14	21

22	29
23	30
24	31
25	
26	
27	
28	

CHOCOLATE SUCCESS

Chocolate melts faster if it is broken into small pieces. The melting process should occur slowly, as chocolate scorches if overheated.

Chocolate 'seizes' if it is over-heated or if it comes in contact with water or steam. To rescue seized chocolate, stir a little cream or vegetable oil into the chocolate until it becomes smooth again.

The container in which choco-late is being melted should be kept uncovered and completely dry. Covering could cause condensation.

Chocolate should be stored in a dry airy place at a temperature of about 16°C/60°F. If stored in unsuitable conditions, the cocoa butter in chocolate may rise to the surface, leaving a white film. A similar discoloration occurs when water condenses on the surface. This often happens to refrigerated chocolates that are too loosely wrapped. Chocolate affected in this way is still suitable for melting, but not for grating.

CITRUS SPONGE PUDDING
Serves 4

1 cup/220 g/7 oz caster sugar
$^{1}/_{2}$ cup/60 g/2 oz self-raising flour
3 tblspn desiccated coconut
1 tblspn finely grated lemon rind
1 tblspn finely grated orange rind
2 tblspn lemon juice
2 tblspn orange juice
2 eggs, separated
125 g/4 oz butter, melted and cooled
1 cup/250 mL/8 fl oz milk

1 Combine sugar, flour, coconut, lemon rind and orange rind in a bowl. Beat in lemon juice, orange juice, egg yolks, butter and milk.

2 Beat egg whites until stiff peaks form and fold into citrus mixture. Pour mixture into a greased 4 cup/1 litre/1$^{3}/_{4}$ pt capacity ovenproof dish. Place in a baking dish, with enough hot water to come halfway up the sides of the dish and bake at 180°C/350°F/Gas 4 for 45 minutes or until cooked.

CHOCOLATE MOUSSE CAKE
Makes a 23 cm/9 in round cake

1 ready-made 23 cm/9 in chocolate
sponge or butter cake
2 tblspn brandy
chocolate mint sticks

MOUSSE FILLING
500 g/1 lb chocolate, chopped
125 g/4 oz butter
2 egg yolks
1¹/₂ cups/375 mL/12 fl oz cream
(double), whipped

1 Filling: Melt chocolate and butter together. Set aside to cool slightly. Beat egg yolks into cooled chocolate mixture, then fold in cream.

2 Using a serrated edged knife, cut cake horizontally into three even layers. Brush each layer with brandy. Place one layer of cake in the base of a lined 23 cm/9 in springform tin. Spoon one-third of the filling over cake in tin. Top with a second layer of cake and half the remaining filling. Repeat layers. Refrigerate for 4 hours or until firm. Decorate with chocolate mint sticks.

PLUM CLAFOUTIS
Serves 6

500 g/1 lb dark plums, halved and stoned,
or 440 g/14 oz canned plums, well drained
1 cup/125 g/4 oz self-raising flour
3 eggs
^{1}/2 cup/100 g/3^1/2 oz caster sugar
^{1}/2 cup/125 mL/4 fl oz reduced-fat milk
1 tblspn icing sugar, sifted

1 Arrange plums, cut side down, in a lightly greased 25 cm/10 in flan dish.

2 Sift flour into a bowl and make a well in the centre. Break eggs into well, add caster sugar and milk and mix to form a smooth batter.

3 Pour batter over plums and bake 180°C/350°F/ Gas 4 for 45 minutes or until firm and golden. Serve hot, warm or cold, sprinkled with icing sugar.

CHOCOLATE PECAN GATEAU
Serves 8

4 eggs, separated
$^3/_4$ cup/170 g/5$^1/_2$ oz caster sugar
2 tblspn brandy
200 g/6$^1/_2$ oz pecans, roughly chopped
2 tblspn flour

CHOCOLATE BRANDY GLAZE
315 g/10 oz milk chocolate
2 tspn instant coffee powder
$^1/_3$ cup/90 mL/3 fl oz cream (double)
1 tblspn brandy
155 g/5 oz pecans, roughly chopped

1 Place egg yolks, sugar and brandy in a bowl and beat until thick and pale. Place egg whites in a clean bowl and beat until stiff peaks form. Fold egg whites, pecans and flour into egg yolk mixture.

2 Pour mixture into a lightly greased and lined 23 cm/9 in springform tin and bake at 160°C/325°F/ Gas 3 for 40 minutes or until cake is firm. Cool in tin.

3 Glaze: Place chocolate, coffee powder, cream and brandy in a heatproof bowl set over a saucepan of simmering water and heat, stirring, until mixture is smooth. Remove bowl from pan and cool slightly. Spread glaze over top and sides of cooled cake. Sprinkle pecans over top of cake and press into sides of cake. Allow to set before serving.

TUILE CUPS WITH WHITE CHOCOLATE
Makes 28

ALMOND TUILE CUPS
125 g/4 oz butter, melted
4 egg whites
2 tblspn milk
1 cup/125 g/4 oz flour
$^2/_3$ cup/140 g/4$^1/_2$ oz caster sugar
60 g/2 oz flaked almonds

WHITE CHOCOLATE FILLING
250 g/8 oz white chocolate,
broken into pieces
60 g/2 oz butter, chopped
$^1/_4$ cup/60 mL/2 fl oz cream (double)

1 Tuile cups: Place butter, egg whites, milk, flour and sugar in a bowl and beat until smooth.

2 Place 2 tspn of mixture on a lightly greased baking tray and spread out to make a 10 cm/4 in round. Repeat with remaining mixture leaving 10 cm/4 in between each tuile. Sprinkle with almonds and bake at 160°C/350°F/Gas 3 for 3-5 minutes or until edges of tuiles are golden. Using a spatula, carefully remove tuiles from trays and place over a small upturned strainer. Press gently to shape. Allow to cool and harden before removing from strainer. Repeat to use remaining mixture.

3 Filling: Place chocolate, butter and cream in a heatproof bowl set over a saucepan of simmering water and heat, stirring, until mixture is smooth. Remove bowl from pan and set aside until mixture thickens slightly. Beat mixture until light and thick. Spoon mixture into a piping bag and pipe into tuile cups.

CASSATA LAYERS
Serves 10

1 ready-made 20 cm/8 in sponge cake
¹/₄ cup/60 mL/2 fl oz almond-flavoured liqueur
chocolate curls

CASSATA FILLING
1 litre/1³/₄ pt vanilla ice cream, softened
1 cup/250 mL/8 fl oz cream (double)
125 g/4 oz glacé apricots, chopped
125 g/4 oz glacé pineapple, chopped
125 g/4 oz glacé cherries, chopped
60 g/2 oz raisins, halved
125 g/4 oz dark chocolate, grated
125 g/4 oz pistachio nuts, chopped

1 Filling: Place ice cream, cream, apricots
pineapple, cherries, raisins, chocolate and pistachio
nuts in a bowl and mix to combine.

2 Split sponge horizontally into three even layers
Place one layer of cake in the base of a lined
20 cm/8 in springform tin and sprinkle with 1 tblspr.
of liqueur. Top with one-third of the filling. Repeat
layers to use all ingredients ending with a layer of
filling. Freeze for 5 hours or until firm. Remove
from freezer 1 hour before serving and place
in refrigerator.

3 Just prior to serving, decorate with chocolate
curls.

WAFFLES WITH CARAMEL APPLES
Serves 4

125 g/4 oz butter
³/₄ cup/125 g/4 oz brown sugar
2 apples, cored, peeled and sliced
¹/₂ cup/125 mL/4 fl oz cream (double)
8 waffles, toasted
4 scoops vanilla ice cream (optional)

1 Melt butter in a frying pan over a medium heat, add sugar and cook, stirring, for 2-3 minutes or until sugar melts and mixture combines.

2 Add apples and cook for 2 minutes. Stir in cream, bring to simmering and simmer for 4 minutes.

3 To serve, place 2 waffles on each serving plate, spoon over apple mixture and accompany with ice cream if desired.

1	8	15
2	9	16
3	10	17
4	11	18
5	12	19
6	13	20
7	14	21

22	*29*
23	*30*
24	
25	
26	
27	
28	

BAKING SECRETS

An accurate oven is essential for successful baking. It should be well insulated and draught proof, as a discrepancy of just a few degrees can ruin baked goods. Regular checking with an oven thermometer helps avoid failures.

A freshly baked cake is very fragile. Allow the cake to cool for a short time in the tin before turning onto a wire rack to cool completely.

Cool cakes on wire racks so that the air can circulate freely around them. This prevents cakes getting soggy in the middle and collapsing.

Allow cakes to cool completely before placing in an airtight container, or condensation will accumulate in the container and cause the cake to go mouldy.

Fat or shortening makes a baked product tender and helps to improve its keeping quality. In most baked goods top quality margarine and butter are interchangeable.

LEMON POPPY SEED MUFFINS
Makes 6

2 eggs, lightly beaten
1 cup/250 g/8 oz sour cream
$^1/_2$ cup/125 mL/4 fl oz milk
$^1/_4$ cup/60 mL/2 fl oz vegetable oil
$^1/_4$ cup/90 g/3 oz honey
3 tblspn poppy seeds
1 tblspn finely grated lemon rind
2$^1/_4$ cups/280 g/9 oz self-raising flour, sifted

LEMON CREAM CHEESE ICING
60 g/2 oz cream cheese, softened
1 tblspn lemon juice
$^3/_4$ cup/125 g/4 oz icing sugar

1 Combine eggs, sour cream, milk, oil, honey, poppy seeds and lemon rind. Add flour and mix until just combined.

2 Spoon mixture into six greased 1 cup/250 mL/8 fl oz capacity muffin tins and bake at 180°C/350°F/Gas 4 for 25-30 minutes or until cooked when tested with a skewer. Turn onto wire racks to cool.

3 Icing: Place cream cheese, lemon juice and icing sugar in a food processor and process until smooth. Top cold muffins with icing.

WHITE JAFFA CAKE
Makes a 23 cm/9 in ring cake

155 g/5 oz white chocolate, chopped
250 g/8 oz butter, chopped
1 cup/250 g/8 oz sugar
3 eggs, lightly beaten
2 tblspn grated orange rind
1 tblspn orange-flavoured liqueur
2¹/₂ cups/315 g/10 oz self-raising flour, sifted
¹/₄ cup/60 mL/2 fl oz milk

1 Melt chocolate. Set aside to cool slightly.

2 Cream butter and sugar. Gradually beat in eggs. Add orange rind, liqueur and cooled chocolate and mix to combine.

3 Mix in flour and milk. Pour mixture into a lightly greased 23 cm/9 in fluted ring tin and bake at 180°C/350°F/Gas 4 for 30 minutes or until cooked when tested with a skewer. Stand cake in tin for 5 minutes before turning onto a wire rack to cool.

december
décembre dezember
diciembre

1	8	15
2	9	16
3	10	17
4	11	18
5	12	19
6	13	20
7	14	21

22	29
23	30
24	31
25	
26	
27	
28	

IMPROMPTU ENTERTAINING

One of the secrets to successful impromptu entertaining is presentation. Remember, to use your good china and cutlery, take a little extra time to arrange food attractively and use simple garnishes.

The addition of a bowl of flowers, fresh fruit or candles gives your dinner table a festive appearance.

For a very simple table decoration place a small flower or herb sprig on each table napkin.

Keep a selection of paper napkins on hand that match your china and you will always be able to colour coordinate your table.

Check out the confectionary and biscuit sections of the supermarket; there are some excellent packaged items that are delicious to have with coffee and are good to have on hand for impromptu entertaining.

ICE CREAM CHRISTMAS PUDDING
Serves 8

1 litre/1³/4 pt chocolate ice cream, softened
125 g/4 oz glacé apricots, chopped
125 g/4 oz glacé cherries, chopped
125 g/4 oz glacé pears, chopped
90 g/3 oz sultanas
75 g/2¹/2 oz raisins, chopped
2 tblspn rum

1 Place ice cream, apricots, cherries, pears, sultanas, raisins and rum in a bowl and mix to combine. Pour into an oiled and lined 6 cup/ 1.5 litre/2¹/2 pt capacity pudding basin.

2 Freeze for 3 hours or until firm.

CHOCOLATE STOCKING BISCUITS
Makes 24

125 g/4 oz butter
$^3/_4$ cup/125 g/4 oz icing sugar
1 egg
$1^1/_4$ cups/155 g/5 oz flour
$1^1/_4$ cups/155 g/5 oz self-raising flour
90 g/3 oz dark chocolate, melted
60 g/2 oz milk chocolate, melted

1 Place butter, icing sugar, egg, flour and self-raising flour in a food processor and process to form a soft dough. Knead briefly, wrap in plastic food wrap and chill for 30 minutes.

2 Roll out dough on nonstick baking paper to 5 mm/$^1/_4$ in thick. Using a template of a Christmas stocking cut out stocking shapes and place on greased baking trays. Bake at 180°C/350°F/Gas 4 for 10 minutes or until biscuits are golden. Cool on wire racks.

3 Dip top of stockings in dark chocolate to make a 1 cm/$^1/_2$ in border. Allow to set. Dip biscuits in milk chocolate halfway up dark chocolate. Allow to set.

INDEX

Food Editor: Rachel Blackmore
Production Manager: Anna Maguire
Design and Layout: Sheridan Packer
Picture Editor: Kirsten Holmes
Trainee Production Editor: Danielle Thiris
Editorial and Production Assistant: Allison Ellul
Recipe Development: Sheryle Eastwood, Lee Gold,
Donna Hay, Jody Vassallo
Photography: Quentin Bacon, Jon Bader,
John Hollingshead, William Meppem
Food Styling: Donna Hay, Liz Nolan, Anna Phillips

Published by J.B. Fairfax Press Pty Limited
80-82 McLachlan Ave
Rushcutters Bay, NSW, Australia, 2011
Ph: (02) 361 6366 Fax: (02) 360 6262
A.C.N. 003 738 430

Formatted by J.B. Fairfax Press Pty Limited
Printed by South China Printing Co, Hong Kong

PRINTED IN HONG KONG

Some of the contents of this book have been previously
published in other J.B. Fairfax Press publications.

JBFP 375
ISBN 1 86343 257 4
ISBN 1 86343 259 0 (collection)